Leeds Un
Quiz Bo

C000061376

101 Questions That Will Test `.
Of This Prestigious Club

Published by Glowworm Press
7 Nuffield Way
Abingdon
Oxfordshire OX14 1RL

By Chris Carpenter

Leeds United Football Club

This book contains one hundred and one informative and entertaining trivia questions with multiple-choice answers. With 101 questions, some easy, some not so easy, this entertaining book will test your knowledge and memory of the club's long and successful history. The book is packed with information and is a must-have for all loyal Leeds supporters. You will be asked questions on a wide range of topics associated with Leeds United Football Club for you to test yourself. You will be quizzed on players, legends, managers, opponents, transfer deals, trophies, records, honours, fixtures, songs and more. Educational, enjoyable and fun, The Leeds United Quiz Book will provide the ultimate in entertainment for **Leeds United** FC fans of all ages, and will test your knowledge to prove you know your LUFC trivia in this fun addictive quiz book.

2019/20 Season Edition

FOREWORD

When I was asked to write a foreword to this book I was incredibly flattered.

I have known the author Chris Carpenter for many years and his knowledge of facts and figures is phenomenal.

His love for football and his talent for writing quiz books makes him the ideal man to pay homage to my great love Leeds United Football Club.

This book came about as a result of a challenge in a Lebanese restaurant of all places!

I do hope you enjoy the book.

Billy Clarke

Let's start off with some relatively easy questions.

1. When were Leeds United founded?
   A. 1909
   B. 1919
   C. 1929

2. What is Leeds United's nickname?
   A. The Roses
   B. The Whites
   C. The Yorkies

3. Where does Leeds United play their home games?
   A. Bramall Lane
   B. Elland Road
   C. Highfield Road

4. What is the stadium's capacity?
   A. 37,890
   B. 38,890
   C. 39,890

5. Who or what is the club mascot?
   A. Lee the Lemur
   B. Lucas the Kop Kat
   C. Whitey the Terrier

6. Who has made the most appearances for the club in total?
   A. Jack Charlton
   B. Norman Hunter
   C. Lucas Radebe

7. Who is the club's record goal scorer?
   A. Lee Chapman
   B. Peter Lorimer
   C. Alan Smith

8. Who is the fastest ever goal scorer for the club?
   A. John Charles
   B. Brian Deane
   C. Mark Viduka

9. What song do the players run out to?
   A. Dance of the Knights
   B. Knights of Cydonia
   C. Night Fever

10. Which of these is a well-known pub near the ground?
    A. The Old Peacock
    B. The White Knight
    C. The Yorkshire Tavern

OK, so here are the answers to the first ten questions. You should get at least seven right, but don't get too cocky, as the questions will get harder.

A1. Leeds United was officially formed in 1919, following the forced disbandment of Leeds City.

A2. The club's nickname is of course the Whites, owing to their all white home strip.

A3. Elland Road has been the club's home ground since their formation in 1919, and has hosted many memorable games in domestic and European competitions.

A4. Although a capacity of 37,890 seems fairly modest, the atmosphere at Elland Road can be incredible when the home fans are in full voice.

A5. Lucas the Kop Kat has roared on Leeds at every home game since 2005.

A6. Leeds and England legend Jack Charlton holds the appearance record, putting on the club's shirt an incredible 773 times. Billy Bremner finished his career only one appearance behind this.

A7. The club's all-time record goal scorer is Peter Lorimer, who netted an impressive 238 goals for the club in all competitions.

A8. Aussie striker Viduka was a fans' favourite during his time at Elland Road, and scored the club's fastest ever goal, netting against Charlton Athletic after just 11 seconds.

A9. Dance of the Knights by Prokofiev blasts out at Elland Road as the mighty whites run out onto the pitch, and the atmosphere is electrified!

A10. The Old Peacock is a boozer opposite the ground that has been frequented by home supporters on match days for many years. Be prepared to queue for a pint though.

OK, back to the questions.

11. What is the highest number of goals that Leeds United has scored in a league season?
    A. 98
    B. 99
    C. 100

12. What is the fewest number of goals that Leeds United has conceded in a league season?
    A. 25
    B. 26
    C. 27

13. Who has scored the most penalties for the club in the Premier League?
    A. Michael Bridges
    B. Ian Harte
    C. Gordon Strachan

14. Who has made the most league appearances for the club?
    A. Billy Bremner
    B. Jack Charlton
    C. John Lukic

15. What is the home end of the ground known as?
    A. John Charles Stand
    B. Revie Stand
    C. South Stand

16. What is the club's record attendance?
    A. 57,289
    B. 57,892
    C. 57,928

17. Where is Leeds United's training ground?
    A. Carrington
    B. Melwood

C. Thorp Arch

18. What is the name of the road the ground is on?
     A. City Road
     B. Elland Road
     C. London Road

19. Which stand has the biggest capacity?
     A. East Stand
     B. South Stand
     C. Revie Stand

20. What is the size of the pitch?
     A. 112x72 yards
     B. 115x74 yards
     C. 118x75 yards

Here is the latest set of answers.

A11. The Whites scored 98 goals in a single season all the way back in the 1927/28 season; something the club's faithful fans would love to see happen again.

A12. Leeds' meanest defensive campaign came in the 1968/69 season, conceding only 26 goals on their way to the First Division title.

A13. Ian Harte and Gordon Strachan jointly hold the record for penalties scored for Leeds in the Premier League, with 10 each.

A14. Defensive rock Jack Charlton made an incredible 629 league appearances for Leeds. Not surprising as he was at the club for his whole professional career.

A15. The Revie Stand is the home end where the bulk of the most diehard fans congregate on match days.

A16. 57,892 fans crammed into Elland Road to see Leeds play Sunderland in an FA Cup 5th round replay in 1967.

A17. Thorp Arch, near the town of Wetherby, is the home of Leeds United's state of the art training facilities.

A18. No excuses for getting this one wrong. The ground is of course on Elland Road.

A19. The East Stand is the newest and largest stand at Elland Road. It was completed in the 1992/93 season and holds 15,100 fans.

A20. At 115 yards long and 74 yards wide, Elland Road boasts one of the largest playing surfaces in the Football League.

Now we move onto some questions about the club's records.

21. What is the club's record win in any competition?
    A. 8-0
    B. 9-0
    C. 10-0

22. Who did they beat?
    A. Molde
    B. Lyn Oslo
    C. Viking Stavanger

23. In which season?
    A. 1969/70
    B. 1970/71
    C. 1971/72

24. What is the club's record win in the league?
    A. 8-0
    B. 9-0
    C. 10-0

25. Who did they beat?
    A. Manchester City
    B. Stoke City
    C. Leicester City

26. In which season?
    A. 1932/33
    B. 1933/34
    C. 1934/35

27. What is the club's record defeat?
    A. 1-8
    B. 2-9
    C. 3-10

28. Who against?

A. Stevenage Borough
B. Stoke City
C. Sunderland

29. In which season?
A. 1934/35
B. 1935/36
C. 1936/37

30. Who has scored the most hat tricks for Leeds United?
A. Allan Clarke
B. Peter Lorimer
C. Both

Here is your latest set of answers.

A21. Leeds United's record victor in any competition is a whopping 10-0 victory. I feel sorry for the opposition goalie.

A22. This huge victory came against Norwegian part-timers Lyn Oslo in the first round of the European Cup.

A23. The game took place on 17th September 1969, so it was thus in the 1969/70 season.

A24. The Whites' biggest margin of victory in the league was an 8-0 win.

A25. This drubbing came against the Foxes of Leicester City, who clearly didn't turn up to play that day.

A26. This record win came on 7th April 1934, so it was thus in the 1933/34 season.

A27. Leeds' record defeat was an embarrassing 1-8 mauling in the League.

A28. This record defeat came at the hands of Stoke City.

A29. The record defeat occurred all the way back on 3rd September 1934 in the 1934/35 season.

A30. There are quite a few Leeds United players who share this particular record. Allan Clarke, Peter Lorimer, Arthur Graham, Lee Chapman, Tony Yeboah and Jermaine Beckford have all scored 3 hat tricks for the club. Give yourself a bonus point if you knew that.

Now we move onto some questions about the club's trophies.

31. When did the club win their first League title?
    A. 1966/67
    B. 1967/68
    C. 1968/69

32. When did the club win their first FA Cup?
    A. 1962
    B. 1972
    C. 1982

33. Who did they beat in the final?
    A. Arsenal
    B. Manchester United
    C. Liverpool

34. What was the score?
    A. 3-0
    B. 2-1
    C. 1-0

35. How many times has Leeds United won the League?
    A. 2
    B. 3
    C. 4

36. How many times have Leeds United won the FA Cup?
    A. 1
    B. 2
    C. 3

37. How many times have they won the League Cup?
    A. 1
    B. 2
    C. 3

38. Who was the last captain to lift the League trophy?

A. Billy Bremner
B. Gary McAllister
C. Gordon Strachan

39. Who was the last captain to lift the FA Cup?
    A. Billy Bremner
    B. Jack Charlton
    C. Paul Madeley

40. Who was the last captain to lift the League Cup?
    A. Billy Bremner
    B. Allan Clarke
    C. Johnny Giles

Here are the set of answers to the last batch of questions.

A31. Leeds lifted their first League title at the end of the 1968/69 season.

A32. The Whites lifted their first FA Cup in 1972, during a period of dominance by the club in English football.

A33. Leeds defeated Arsenal on 6th May 1972 at Wembley, in the Centenary Cup Final.

A34. Leeds edged a close final 1-0 thanks to a diving header scored in the 54th minute by star striker Allan Clarke.

A35. The Whites have lifted the League championship on three occasions, but never in the Premier League era.

A36. Surprisingly, Leeds has only managed to capture the FA cup once in their illustrious history.

A37. The League Cup has also only been in the Elland Road trophy room on one occasion.

A38. Fiery Scotsman Gordon Strachan was the captain as Leeds lifted the Division One trophy at the end of the 1991/92 season, the final season before the birth of the Premier League.

A39. The most successful captain in the club's history; Billy Bremner had the captain's armband when Leeds won the FA Cup in 1972.

A40. That man again, Billy Bremner was also the captain for Leeds' only League Cup triumph, lifting the trophy in 1968.

I hope you're having fun, and getting most of the answers right.

41. What is the record transfer fee paid?
    A. £8 million
    B. £18 million
    C. £28 million

42. Who was the record transfer fee paid for?
    A. Tony Yeboah
    B. Rio Ferdinand
    C. Robbie Keane

43. What is the record transfer fee received?
    A. £30.8 million
    B. £31.8 million
    C. £32.8 million

44. Who was the record transfer fee received for?
    A. Harry Kewell
    B. Rio Ferdinand
    C. Jonathan Woodgate

45. Who was the first Leeds United player to play for England?
    A. John Charles
    B. Jack Charlton
    C. Willis Edwards

46. Who has won the most international caps whilst a Leeds United player?
    A. Johnny Giles
    B. Harry Kewell
    C. Lucas Radebe

47. Who has scored the most international goals whilst a Leeds United player?
    A. Lee Chapman
    B. Allan Clarke

C. Peter Lorimer

48. Who is the youngest player ever to represent the club?
    A. Fabian Delph
    B. Peter Lorimer
    C. James Milner

49. Who is the club's youngest ever goalscorer?
    A. Michael Bridges
    B. Gary Kelly
    C. James Milner

50. Who is the oldest player ever to represent the club?
    A. Eddie Burbanks
    B. Freddie Maybanks
    C. Teddy Sandbanks

Here are the set of answers to the last set of questions.

A41. The most Leeds has paid for a single player is £18 million.

A42. Rio Ferdinand made the headlines when Leeds paid West Ham United £18 million for his services in November 2000. This was the highest fee paid for a teenager at this time.

A43. The highest amount Leeds has received for a single player in their history is £30.8 million.

A44. The club ended up making a tidy profit when selling Rio Ferdinand to rivals Manchester United in July 2002, although the sale only happened to save the club from administration and balance the books.

A45. Club legend Willis Edwards was the first Leeds United player to be capped by England. He made 16 appearances for his country as well as 444 games for the Whites.

A46. A strong centre-back known as 'Chief" during his time at Elland Road, Lucas Radebe made 61 appearances for South Africa while playing for Leeds.

A47. Allan Clarke scored all 10 of his England goals while playing for Leeds.

A48. Peter Lorimer's fantastic career with the Whites started very early. He made his senior debut aged just 15 years and 289 days against Southampton in September 1962.

A49. James Milner seems to have been around forever, and proof of this is his record as Leeds United's youngest ever goal scorer, netting in the Premier League aged just 16 years and 355 days on the 26th December 2002.

A50. The record of The Whites' oldest player goes to Eddie Burbanks, who was 41 year and 23 days old when he played against Hull City in 1954.

I hope you're learning some new facts about the club.

51. What is the club's official twitter account?
    A. @Leeds
    B. @LeedsUnited
    C. @lufc

52. Who is the club's longest serving manager of all time?
    A. George Graham
    B. Dick Ray
    C. Don Revie

53. Who is the club's longest serving post war manager?
    A. Brian McDermott
    B. David O'Leary
    C. Don Revie

54. What is the name of the Leeds United match day programme?
    A. Marching On Together
    B. The Super Whites
    C. We Are Leeds

55. What is the highest number of players used in a single season?
    A. 40
    B. 42
    C. 44

56. Which of these is a Leeds United fanzine?
    A. Marching On Together
    B. Leeds, Leeds, Leeds
    C. The Square Ball

57. What animal/symbol/motif is on the club crest?
    A. An Owl
    B. A Peacock
    C. A Rose and Ball on a Shield

58. What is the club's motto?
    A. Arte et Labore
    B. Pro rege et lege
    C. Superbia in Proelia

59. Who is considered as Leeds United's main rivals?
    A. Bradford City
    B. Galatasaray
    C. Manchester United

60. What could be regarded as the club's most well-known song?
    A. Eye of the Tiger
    B. Glory Glory Leeds United
    C. Marching On Together

Here are the answers to the last set of questions.

A51. @LUFC is the official twitter account of the club. It tweets multiple times a day, and it deserves far more followers than it has.

A52. United's longest serving (and most successful) manager is club legend Don Revie, who is still considered a god amongst the Leeds faithful.

A53. Again Don Revie holds this record. He was at the helm for 13 glorious years.

A54. Fans eagerly devour the information held within the match day programme We Are Leeds before every home game.

A55. Incredibly, 44 players were used during the 2006/07 season, the season the club finished bottom of the Football League Championship. Those were dark days.

A56. The Square Ball is Leeds' fans most popular fanzine, and was voted Fanzine of the Year in 2011 by the Football Supporters Federation.

A57. The club has changed its crest many times over the years, but the current edition features the white rose of Yorkshire and a ball on a shield.

A58. The club shares its motto with the city of Leeds. "Pro rege et lege" which translates to "For the King and the Law".

A59. Leeds are rivals to a number of clubs for various geographical and footballing reasons, but their bitterest rivals are their enemies from over the Pennines, Manchester United. A real war of the roses.

A60. Marching On Together (Leeds Leeds Leeds) has been the club's anthem since the 1970s and is still bellowed from the stands at every match.

Let's give you some easier questions.

61. What is the traditional colour of the home shirt?
    A. Red
    B. Blue
    C. White

62. What is the traditional colour of the away shirt?
    A. Green
    B. Red
    C. Yellow

63. Who is the current club shirt sponsor?
    A. 32Red
    B. 888Bet
    C. Bet365

64. Who was the first club sponsor?
    A. Burton
    B. RF Winders
    C. Strongbow

65. Which of these hotel chains once sponsored the club?
    A. Hilton Hotels
    B. Thistle Hotels
    C. Travelodge

66. Who is currently the club chairman?
    A. Massimo Cellino
    B. Ken Bates
    C. Andrea Radrizzani

67. Who was the club's first foreign signing?
    A. Allan Harvey
    B. Eric Cantona
    C. Eirik Bakke

68. Who was the club's first black player?

    A. Lucas Radebe
    B. Albert Johanneson
    C. Tony Yeboah

69. Who was the club's first ever match in the league against?
    A. Portsmouth
    B. Port Vale
    C. Plymouth Argyle

70. Who are the club's current kit manufacturers?
    A. Admiral
    B. Kappa
    C. Macron

Here are the set of answers to the last set of questions.

A61. Don Revie changed the club shirts to all white in imitation of Real Madrid when he took over the helm, and the club has been famous for this colour ever since.

A62. Most of Leeds United's away kits have incorporated yellow shirts since the Don Revie Era, possibly emulating another footballing superpower, Brazil.

A63. Online casino company 32Red is the current club sponsor.

A64. RF Winders, a local company, were the first ever business to sponsor the Leeds shirt in 1983.

A65. From 1993 to 1996 Leeds were sponsored by Thistle Hotels.

A66. Leeds fans are hopeful that the current chairman Italian Andrea Radrizzani can bring some stability to the club after a very turbulent few years for the club.

A67. Alan Harvey made history as the first foreigner to play for Leeds United. The Canadian spent one season at the club in 1959/60.

A68. Albert Johanneson was the first black footballer to play for Leeds United, and one of the first black players to players to play in the top-flight.

A69. Leeds played their first ever league match against Port Vale on the 28th August 1920 and lost 2-0.

A70. Kappa are the current kit supplier to the club.

Ok, on with the questions, how are you doing so far?

71. Who is Leeds United's highest goal scorer in the Premier League?
    A. Harry Kewell
    B. Alan Smith
    C. Mark Viduka

72. What is Leeds United's highest Premier League finish?
    A. 3rd
    B. 4th
    C. 6th

73. Which Leeds United player holds the record for most goals in a season?
    A. John Charles
    B. Allan Clarke
    C. Tony Yeboah

74. Which other Norwegian player did Eirik Bakke replace in centre midfield for Leeds United?
    A. Morten Gamst Pederson
    B. Tore Andre Flo
    C. Alf Inge-Haaland

75. What is Leeds United's biggest win in a friendly match?
    A. 15-0
    B. 16-0
    C. 17-0

76. When was the club's worst ever finish in English football?
    A. 2007/08
    B. 2008/09
    C. 2009/10

77. How many games did Leeds United go unbeaten from the start of the 1973/74 season?

A. 29
B. 30
C. 31

78. Which Leeds United player scored the most goals in a single game?
    A. Gordon Hodgson
    B. Mark Viduka
    C. Rod Wallace

79. What is Leeds United's lowest goal total in a Premier League season?
    A. 28
    B. 38
    C. 48

80. How many Leeds United players have won the PFA Players' Player of the Year?
    A. 0
    B. 1
    C. 2

Here are the set of answers to the last block of questions.

A71. Skilful Australian striker Mark Viduka is the Whites' top premier league marksman, netting 59 times in three seasons with Leeds in the top flight.

A72. Leeds' highest finish in the Premier League was an impressive 3rd in the 1999/2000 season, but things sadly began to fall apart for them afterwards.

A73. Wales and Leeds legend John Charles scored an incredible 42 goals in the 1953/54 season, making him the club's most prolific scorer in a single season.

A74. Eirik Bakke succeeded Fellow Norwegian Alf Inge-Haaland in the Leeds midfield. He went on to represent Manchester City in the Premier League.

A75. Leeds destroyed FC Gherdeina 16-0 in a pre-season friendly in 2004. There's nothing friendly about the score-line in that match though.

A76. At the end of the 2007/08 season, Leeds finished in 5th positon in League One, the third tier of English football. This is the club's worst ever finish.

A77. Don Revie's legendary team went 29 matches unbeaten at the start of the 1973/74 season, a record for the club.

A78. A club legend between the two world wars, Gordon Hodgson scored 5 goals in a match against Leicester in 1938.

A79. Watching Leeds in the 1996/97 season wasn't always that exciting. The club only managed to find the net 28 times in 38 games.

A80. Just one Leeds player has been honoured by his fellow professionals with the PFA Players' Player award. Norman Hunter collected the trophy in 1973/74.

Here's the next batch of questions.

81. Which former Leeds United player had a less than memorable debut in La Liga?
    A. Jimmy Floyd Hasselbaink
    B. Ian Harte
    C. Jonathan Woodgate

82. Which Leeds United player missed a crucial penalty for England against Argentina at the 1998 World Cup?
    A. David Batty
    B. Paul Robinson
    C. Jason Wilcox

83. Which Leeds United player scored the club's first Premier League hat trick?
    A. Eric Cantona
    B. Lee Chapman
    C. Robbie Fowler

84. Who was Leeds United's first non-British player to be voted Player of the Season?
    A. Albert Johanneson
    B. Gary Kelly
    C. Tony Yeboah

85. Which legendary manager was appointed at Leeds United, only to be sacked 44 days later?
    A. Sir Matt Busby
    B. Brian Clough
    C. Bill Shankly

86. Against which Football League club has Leeds United played most times in their history?
    A. Leicester City
    B. Manchester City
    C. Swansea City

87. Who was voted Leeds United's greatest ever goalkeeper?
    A. Nigel Martyn
    B. John Lukic
    C. Gary Sprake

88. Against who was Leeds United's last major cup final?
    A. Arsenal
    B. Aston Villa
    C. Anderlecht

89. Who is the only Leeds United Player to win the Premier League Golden Boot?
    A. Robbie Fowler
    B. Jimmy Floyd Hasselbaink
    C. Mark Viduka

90. Which Leeds goalkeeper scored one of the most calamitous own goals of all time?
    A. John Lukic
    B. Paul Robinson
    C. Gary Sprake

Here are the set of answers to the last batch of questions.

A81. Jonathan Woodgate didn't exactly cover himself in glory on 22nd September 2005 - his Spanish league debut scoring an own goal and getting sent off for Real Madrid.

A82. Midfielder David Batty missed an important penalty against Argentina sending England crashing out of the World Cup in France in 1998. His dad was quoted as saying he knew he'd miss it.

A83. Mercurial Frenchman Eric Cantona scored the first hat trick of the Premier League era in August 1992. If only Leeds could have held onto him.

A84. Leeds cult hero Tony Yeboah was the first non-British Player of the Season award, claiming the prize in his second season with the club.

A85. Brian Clough took over from Don Revie but was sacked 44 days later after a disastrous start to the season. He had famously been critical of his new players when he was in charge of Derby County.

A86. Leeds has matched up against Leicester City 110 times in the league over the years.

A87. Cornish shot-stopper Nigel Martyn was voted the Whites' best ever goalkeeper, despite winning no major honours during his six seasons between the sticks. However, he was a consistent performer and a large factor in Leeds' relative success at home and abroad.

A88. Leeds' last appearance in a major cup final came in the 1996 League Cup Final against Aston Villa. However there was no joy for the Elland Road faithful, as Leeds lost the game 3-0.

A89. Dutch striker Jimmy Floyd Hasselbaink captured the Premier League Golden Boot in the 1998/99 season, with his 18 goals helping Leeds to a very respectable 4th place in the table.

A90. Gary Sprake holds this dubious honour, managing to throw the ball behind him into his own net against Liverpool. Every time he returned to Anfield after this, he was greeted by Des O'Connor's 'Careless Hands' over the PA system.

Ok, the last set of questions. Ready? Then, here we go.

91. What relation are Leeds legends Gary Kelly and Ian Harte?
    A. Cousins
    B. Half brothers
    C. Uncle and nephew

92. Against which team did Alan Smith score with his first touch as a professional footballer?
    A. Everton
    B. Liverpool
    C. Manchester United

93. TV presenter Gabby Logan is the daughter of which former Leeds United player?
    A. Jimmy Armfield
    B. Eddy Gray
    C. Terry Yorath

94. What was the club reportedly spending £11,000 per month on during the disastrous financial period when Peter Ridsdale was chairman?
    A. Horse placentas to treat injuries
    B. Spiritual mediums
    C. Tropical fish for the boardroom

95. Which famous Leeds band is named after Lucas Radebe's former club in his home country, South Africa?
    A. Black Star Liner
    B. Kaiser Chiefs
    C. Wild Beasts

96. Which former Spice Girl is a self-confessed Leeds United fan?
    A. Emma Bunton
    B. Mel B
    C. Mel C

97. Why did combative midfielder Lee Bowyer get sent off in a match whilst playing for Newcastle United?
    A. Fighting with the referee
    B. Fighting with a team mate
    C. Fighting with an opposition supporter

98. Which famous actor portrayed Brian Clough in the film "The Damned United" that charted his ill-fated 44 days in charge of Leeds United?
    A. Charlie Sheen
    B. Martin Sheen
    C. Michael Sheen

99. Who started the 2019/2020 season as manager?
    A. Marcelo Bielsa
    B. Paul Heckingbottom
    C. Garry Monk

100.   Who is considered by many to be Leeds United's worst ever signing?
    A. Roque Junior
    B. Lee Sharpe
    C. Paul Rachubka

101.   Which Leeds United manager is honoured with a statue outside Elland Road?
    A. Brian Clough
    B. David O'Leary
    C. Don Revie

Here is the last set of answers.

A91. Defensive stalwarts during Leeds' best period in the Premier League, Irish pair Gary Kelly and Ian Harte are in fact uncle and nephew. Small world, huh?

A92. Local boy and club hero Alan Smith scored with his first ever touch against league rivals Liverpool. What a start to a career!

A93. Terry Yorath was a member of the 1973/74 title winning side. He is also the father of broadcaster Gabby Logan, who was Gabby Yorath before her marriage to rugby player Kenny.

A94. During the club's financial meltdown of the early 2000's, it was reported that £11,000 a month was being squandered on tropical fish for the boardroom. Madness.

A95. It is The Kaiser Chiefs that are named after Lucas Radebe's first professional team.

A96. Leeds lass Scary Spice Mel B is one of the club's most famous supporters, although being based in Los Angeles these days she doesn't get to see many games.

A97. Among several moments of controversy in his career, Lee Bowyer was dismissed in one match for fighting with a player on his own team, Newcastle United team mate Kieron Dyer.

A98. Welsh actor Michael Sheen played Clough in the movie, although the idea of Charlie Sheen having a go is quite appealing.

A99. Marcelo Bielsa started the 2019/20 season as manger having been appointed in June 2018. Based on the merry go round of managers in recent years, it's anyone's guess if he will still be there at the end of the season.

A100. World Cup winner Roque Junior was signed to try and plug the holes in the Leeds defence as they fought relegation during the 2003/04 season. In the 7 games he played in central defence, Leeds conceded 24 goals.

A101. Who else but the most successful manager in the club's history? Don Revie has been immortalised in bronze with a statue outside Leeds' home ground.

That's it. I hope you enjoyed this book, and I hope you got most of the answers right. I also hope you learnt one or two new things about the club.

Thanks for reading, and if you did enjoy the book, would you be so kind as leave a positive review on Amazon.

Printed in Great
Britain
by Amazon